The 1899 Newsboys' STRIKE

BY NEL YOMTOV

ILLUSTRATED BY SILVIO DB

CAPSTONE PRESS
a capstone imprint

TABLE OF CONTENTS

KIDS AT WORK

During the 1800s, it was common for young children in the United States to work. Children as young as six years old worked in factories, coal mines, and mills.

Working conditions were often crowded, unclean, and dangerous. Children were paid less than adults. They were also less likely to join or form unions. Unions helped workers demand better working conditions and wages.

Tens of thousands of children were sent by their parents to work in other people's homes. They worked as maids, servants, farmhands, and helpers of all kinds.

The children earned money to help their families pay their bills.

The young workers represented all walks of life and ethnicities. Many were poor immigrants.

Some lived at home with their families. Others were orphans and runaways who lived on the streets.

In larger cities such as New York and Chicago, child workers had a wide range of street jobs. Kids collected used bottles, rags, and cans to sell for pennies. Some loaded and unloaded trucks or railroad cars.

Others shined shoes, sold candy and gum, delivered packages, or ran messages.

There ya go, mister! Best shine in town!

More boys than girls worked street jobs. Adults made more effort to protect young girls from the roughness of street life.

Working girls cleaned homes, washed laundry, and sewed clothing. Many were paid to take care of babies and younger children.

Hundreds of thousands of boys sold newspapers on city streets all across the United States.

And in the summer of 1899, the "newsboys" themselves would make headlines around the country.

The newsboys were also called "newsies." Newsies ranged in age from 7 or 8 years old to elderly. The average newsie began work as a young teenager.

Get your afternoon paper!

Don't miss today's news! Big fire in warehouse on 23rd Street!

Here ya go, old-timer.

Newsies who attended school worked in the afternoons and evenings. Those who didn't often sold morning, afternoon, and evening editions of newspapers, working from dawn to dusk.

Selling newspapers on the street could be exciting. The noise of trolleys and horse-drawn wagons mixed with the rapid movement of people on the streets.

For many newsies, working outdoors was a relief from small, stuffy apartments and cramped classrooms.

W-whoa! Get your morning news here!

KLANG! KLANG!

K-LUMP K-LUMP

Newsies were self-employed. They worked for themselves.

Hawking papers was difficult. Newsies worked long hours in all weather conditions: rain, snow, frigid cold, and blistering heat. They were on their feet all day with little rest.

Most newsies made only about 25 cents a day, or about $8 in today's money.

Newsies peddled their papers wherever there were the most people. In big cities like New York, they worked the financial districts and large department stores. Others set up shop at the entrances to subway stations and streetcar stops.

Newsies were indispensable to the newspaper industry and the publishers who printed the papers. They were the main means of newspaper sales throughout a city. Home delivery of newspapers was limited. There also were not enough newsstands to serve the city's large population.

Each day, newsies bought papers from newspaper publishers at distribution points around the city. They got the money to buy the papers from their previous day's sales.

The newsies paid 50 cents for 100 papers, or one-half cent per copy. Newsies sold each paper for 1 cent. They made only half a penny on each paper they sold.

Newsies had to plan carefully because they could not return unsold papers. If they bought more than they could sell, they lost money. If they bought too few, they might lose customers who usually bought from the same newsie at the same spot each day.

Most newsies sold the newspapers of different publishers.

Lemme have 200 today, Charlie!

Gimme a bundle of 100!

I wish we could get refunds for copies we don't sell.

Settle down, will ya! There's plenty of copies for all of you!

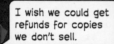

At the end of the 1800s, New York City's two largest newspapers—the *New York World* and the *New York Journal*—were owned by two of the richest and most powerful people in the United States. Joseph Pulitzer owned the *World*, and William Randolph Hearst owned the *Journal*.

During the Spanish-American War in 1898, there was an increased demand for newspapers. Pulitzer and Hearst took advantage of the higher demand and raised the newsboys' cost of 100 papers from 50 cents to 60 cents. Now the newsies made less than half a cent per paper.

At first, the newsies didn't mind the price increase. News of the war fueled brisk sales of their papers. Business was booming.

These are selling faster than hotcakes!

I shoulda bought more to sell!

I'll take two copies today, Sid.

Thanks, lady!

By the summer of 1899, the war headlines faded away. Newsies sold fewer papers.

They expected—and asked—the two publishers to roll back the price to the original 50 cents for 100 copies.

You're my managing editor, Phil. Tell those kids no dice: I refuse to lower the price.

Yessir, Mr. Hearst.

With their livelihood threatened, the newsies grew angry.

I tell ya, it ain't right! They don't wanna raise the price of the paper to their customers, so they're stickin' it to us!

We gotta do somethin'!

Yeah, but what can a bunch of kids do against these fat cats?

STRIKE!

No one is certain where or how the newsboys' strike began. The first recorded action occurred on July 18, 1899, in Long Island City, a community across the East River from Manhattan.

After paying for full bundles, the newsies discovered that the *Journal* deliverymen had shorted the bundles. Their frustration boiled over into violence.

The newsies' bold first action was only the beginning of a larger movement to come.

Minutes later, at Greenpoint Avenue . . .

We gotta make a stand against the *World* and the *Journal*. Force them to put our price back to 50 cents.

I'm with ya, Will. Let's spread the word to the other guys.

News of the Long Island action spread like wildfire through word of mouth and leaflets the newsies handed out. The next day, July 19, hundreds of newsies from across the city gathered in City Hall Park in Lower Manhattan.

Organize! Organize!

Let's show 'em we won't back down!

We're gonna form a union and tell Pulitzer and Hearst we'll strike if they don't roll back the prices!

We'll show 'em!

Let's do it!

Strike! Strike!

But I need the money. I can't strike for long.

If we stick together, they'll have to give in! We'll win quick!

Hearst and Pulitzer refused to give in to the newsies' demand. As a result, the newsboy strike officially began on July 20.

Let's see how many papers they'll sell without us!

As *Journal* and *World* delivery trucks left the papers' printing plants at Park Row, strikers pelted the wagons with rocks, bottles, and fruit. The newsies grabbed copies of the newspapers from the trucks and destroyed them. Police were nearly helpless to stop the chaos.

The newsies' anger was also directed against non-strikers who were still selling the two papers.

Get the scab!

Grab his papers and rip 'em to shreds!

Crews of unruly newsies ran through Park Row, loudly declaring the strike was on.

We don't sell no *World*s or *Journal*s!

We mean business! We won't stand for anyone going against the strike!

Within two days, the strike had spread outside the city—Mount Vernon to the north, and even Jersey City, New Jersey, to the west.

On the afternoon of July 20, strikers marched down Wall Street in the city's financial district. They hoped to gain public support for their cause.

From windows high above the street, businessmen tossed down coins to the strikers as a show of support. They knew the sooner the newsboys returned to work, the sooner they could buy their favorite papers again.

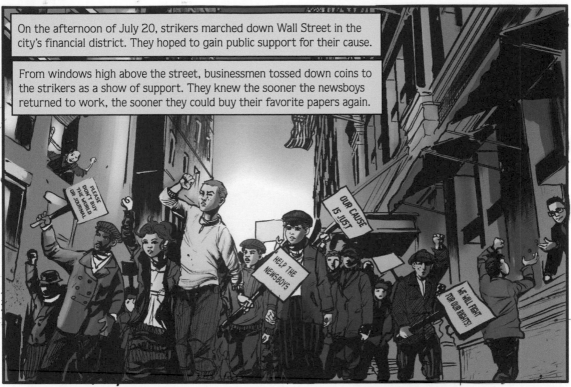

By July 22, the two papers were already feeling the pinch of lost newspaper sales. That day, *World* publisher Joseph Pulitzer heard the grim news from the paper's managing editor, Don Seitz.

The newsboys' strike has grown into a menacing affair, Mr. Pulitzer. It is posing a serious problem.

Practically all the boys in New York City and nearby towns have quit selling.

Two days later, Seitz informed Pulitzer that advertisers had abandoned the papers and sales had dropped 40 percent.

On Manhattan's Lower East Side, strikers turned over a newsstand where the *Journal* and the *World* were being sold. The police arrived, but the newsies escaped easily.

Try to catch me, old man!

At 59th Street and 9th Avenue, one of the distribution points for evening papers, newsies attacked policemen who had been stationed there to protect the delivery wagons.

Though the newsies were only young boys, they were not afraid to commit acts of violence and destruction.

To try to break the strike, Hearst and Pulitzer hired adults to sell their papers for $2 a day.

The newsies responded with a strong show of force. It was becoming impossible for anyone to buy a copy of the *Journal* or the *World* on the city streets.

Unnhhff!

The bigger they are, the harder they fall, eh, boys?

One morning, strikers were waiting for Hearst outside the *Journal* office building when he arrived for work.

We're the strikers, Mr. Hearst. We want 100 papers for 50 cents.

Come up to my office to talk, boys.

I'm Kid Blink, one of the leaders of the strike. Are you gonna lower the price of the bundles? Or buy back our unsold copies?

Hmm. Maybe we can work this out. I'll give you an answer soon.

The strikers never heard back from Hearst.

Police arrested several strikers for disturbing the peace or beating up scabs. Yet the strike was gaining ground. Newsies in many towns and cities outside New York City had also begun to strike.

Leave the kid alone, copper!

Go pick on someone your own size!

The strikers would soon show the entire country just how much they meant business.

THE BIG RALLY

On the evening of July 24, the newly formed Newsboy Strike Committee held a massive rally at New Irving Hall on Broome Street.

More than 5,000 strikers from the city and beyond attended the gathering. A local politician who believed in the newsies' cause helped pay for the rally.

The first speaker of the evening was a lawyer named Leonard Suitkin. He came as a representative of a local assemblyman. The assemblyman supported the strike because he believed the newsies were being treated unfairly by the two papers.

The first striking newsie to speak was 21-year-old Dave Simons, president of the newly formed Newsboys' Union. Simons read a set of resolutions that was addressed to the public.

Please don't buy the *World* or *Journal* until the owners meet our demands.

If you want your news, you'll find it in the *Evening Sun*, *Telegram*, and *Daily News*. They give us a chance to make a living.

Hooray! Hooray! Hooray!

We're with you, Davey Boy!

We're goin' to win this fight, boys, only we must stick together and hold firm.

Now, I'm goin' to ask you not to use no more violence. Let up on the scabs.

Boo! Boo!

Now, I mean it. We can't gain nothing by banging these fellers around.

Let's fight on the level and see if we can't win out that way.

Bob Stone was the next striking newsie to speak.

I'm here to support the union. I want this strike to keep goin' until we win.

Yeah, Bob, yeah!

Strike! Strike!

What do you think Hearst said today? He said he can't afford to sell two papers for a cent. Honest, ain't that sickening?

Haha! Haha!

What a jerk!

Stone concluded his speech with another appeal for nonviolence.

I'm telling you not to soak the drivers anymore. We're goin' to try to succeed without violence. So keep cool.

Next up was 18-year-old Kid Blink, the most well-known leader of the strike. Newspapers quoted him daily. To the public, Kid Blink was the "face" of the newsboys' strike.

You know me, boys. If we're goin' to win this strike, we must stick together like glue and never give up.

We know ya, Kid!

Yes! Yes!

Ain't that ten cents worth as much to us as it is to Hearst and Pulitzer, who are millionaires? Well, I guess it is.

If they can't spare it, how can we?

Yes! Yes!

You bet it is, Kid!

The strikers were fired up to continue striking. As the *Sun* reported, "Then the boys left the hall, yelling like demons, and spent the rest of the evening celebrating the successful strike and their great meeting."

We're gonna win this!

Woo-hoo!

Yeah! Yeah!

Long live the union!

"SAY, WE'RE WINNIN' EASY!"

The newsboy strike made headlines across the United States. Newsies in Connecticut, Rhode Island, and Massachusetts went on strike as a show of support for New York City newsies.

NEWSBOYS' WORDS STAND
They Still Refuse to Sell Papers They Have Boycotted...
THE MORNING NEWS - SAVANNAH -GA

NEWSBOYS' STRIKE
New York, July 23 - The Newsboys' strike against the *Evening World* and the *Evening Journal* is spreading...
DAILY LEADER - MARIETTAM -OH

NEWSBOY STRIKE STRENGTHENS
Newsdealers Agree to Support Their Boycott...
RICHMOND TIMES -VIRGINIA

HOOTED BY NEWSBOYS
Editor Hearst's Unpleasant Experience With Young Strikers...
THE SAN FRANCISCO CALL

The newsies in New York City continued to push for public support. At 3rd Avenue and 5th Street in Manhattan . . .

Gimme that paper!

You little thief!

Give me one reason I shouldn't get a policeman here!

Y—you don't understand, mister. My union is striking the *Journal* and the *World* cuz of the bad way they're treatin' us newsboys.

Sure, I've heard about you kids. Sorry I got mad. Here's a dime for your strike fund.

Thanks, mister. You're a pal!

Aren't you boys angry this girl is selling the papers you're striking?

That's all right, boss. We can't help it. We ain't fightin' women.

Soon, public sympathy was totally on the side of the strikers.

As the days passed, the strike continued to hit the two publishers hard. Sales of the *Journal* and the *World* fell by two-thirds.

Find their leaders and offer them a compromise, Phil. We'll charge them 55 cents per hundred papers instead of 60 cents.

Will do, Mr. Hearst.

The strikers turned down the offer.

Meanwhile, other New York City newspapers benefited from the sagging sales of the *Journal* and the *World*. In the pressroom of the *Evening Telegram* . . .

We've become more popular than ever. I hear our sales are at an all-time high!

We can't print 'em fast enough!

Though the strikers' violence had decreased, the threat of violence had not.

You hear the news? All us *World* delivery drivers are planning to go out on strike today. You with us?

Count me in. I'm not risking my life just to deliver a load of newspapers!

On July 24, a meeting was held at the Westside Newsdealers' Association. The group encouraged the sale of local newspapers and worked for high standards of journalism.

The demands of the strikers are just. We ask every newsdealer in New York City to stop handling the *Journal* and the *World*--and for readers to stop buying them.

Hearst and Pulitzer were desperate. To break the strike, they tried to bribe the strikers with free papers.

Free papers to all you boys who want to sell them! Compliments of Mr. Hearst and the *Journal!*

Gimme two bundles! I'll sell 'em all!

The scheme didn't work.

This'll show those crooks they can't break our strike!

The papers began offering cash bribes to the strikers. Some of the newsies were even visited at their homes.

Everyone's got a price, Duffy. How much to return to work?

I'd rather starve than do my boys out of their jobs. Get outta here!

More desperate than ever, the two papers continued their attempts to bribe the newsies. One newsie reported he was offered $500 to quit the strike. And the *New York Herald* reported, "All through Park Row yesterday could be seen the flash of the crisp new bills."

I haven't earned a dime since we started striking. I don't have enough money to buy a meal.

Here's a dollar. We have to stick this out to the end.

The strike was holding together. All the newsies who were approached with cash bribes refused them.

Except two . . .

BETRAYAL . . . AND SUCCESS!

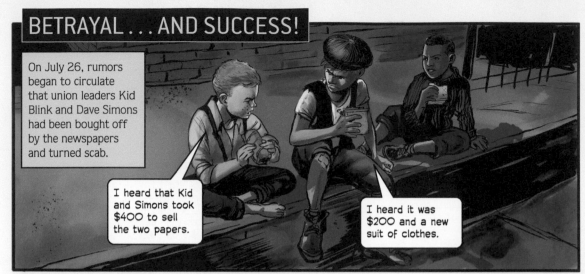

On July 26, rumors began to circulate that union leaders Kid Blink and Dave Simons had been bought off by the newspapers and turned scab.

I heard that Kid and Simons took $400 to sell the two papers.

I heard it was $200 and a new suit of clothes.

Yeah, well I heard it was free papers and a dollar a day!

Some of the boys said it wasn't even a bribe that got them selling again. They said Kid Blink thought the strike was over!

Of all the crazy things!

Strikers tracked down Blink and Simons and brought them in to be tried in "court."

You've been accused of trying to break the strike and with being bribed with $400.

I'm innocent, and that's no lie.

I'm the same--I didn't turn against you boys.

In the end, the "jury" found Blink and Simons innocent. Still, they were removed from their roles as union leaders.

But the former union leaders' troubles weren't over. The next day, newsies spotted the two on Park Row. Kid Blink was wearing a brand-new suit.

Get the scabs!

They lied! They betrayed us!

Wreck Kid's new suit!

Moments later, police arrived and saw the boys running.

So you're the one that's leading this mob! You're under arrest!

Ya dirty scab! I hope they lock ya up!

You're lucky we didn't get our hands on you, Blink!

Kid Blink was charged with disorderly conduct. The next day, he paid a $3 fine and left the court with his mother.

Pulitzer and Hearst grew more frustrated with each passing hour. They claimed the police department was supporting the strikers.

Can you believe this? The *World* and the *Journal* accusing us of helping the strikers!

Saying we're being too easy on the newsies.

The papers must be getting real desperate, chief.

Meanwhile, the strike showed no signs of slowing down as it took on new leadership.

Six thousand strikers took to the streets, cheered by thousands of people who supported their cause.

"Their position is growing steadily stronger," reported the *Morning Telegram*.

SUPPORT OUR CAUSE

KIDS FIGHT FOR RIGHTS

STRIKE

OUR CAUSE IS JUST

HELP THE NEWSBOYS

Nearly two weeks had passed. Finally, in Joseph Pulitzer's office . . .

The loss in circulation has been colossal, sir. It really is remarkable the success these boys have had.

It's time to end this affair, Mr. Seitz. We've lost.

Hearst and Pulitzer admitted defeat. The newsies' strike against the *Journal* and the *World* ended on August 2, 1899, with a compromise.

The price of the papers would remain at 60 cents for 100 papers, but both publishers agreed to take back and refund all unsold copies.

The strikers had achieved their main bargaining goal—being able to sell back unsold papers. They went back to work immediately.

Newsboys' Boycott Over

For two weeks in the summer of 1899, a group of city kids formed a massive movement. The newsies took on and won against two of the richest and most powerful people in the United States.

The young activists showed the world that children could organize and bring about important changes in society.

MORE ABOUT THE 1899 NEWSBOYS' STRIKE

- Did Kid Blink and Dave Simons actually betray the strike? Some evidence raises doubt on the idea that the two newsies turned scab. The details of the betrayal are shaky at best. Some sources say they accepted $400 to sell papers, others say it was $200 and new clothing. Still others give differing accounts. Some historians believe these rumors were spread by the *Journal* and the *World* to create hostility among the strikers, break up the union, and end the strike.

- The newsboys' union did not survive. It had done important work spreading the word, organizing parades and the big rally, and gaining public support. But the strike was really conducted by a loose association of many small groups of strikers who were loyal to local leaders. Once the strike was in full swing, the citywide central union had little power.

- The newsboy strike of 1899 was the fifth in New York City history. Other strikes had occurred as early as 1886, and additional strikes followed until the mid-1900s. The 1899 strike is credited with inspiring later newsboy strikes in Philadelphia and Pittsburgh, Pennsylvania; Boston, Massachusetts; Cincinnati, Ohio; Butte, Montana; Lexington and Louisville, Kentucky; and other places.

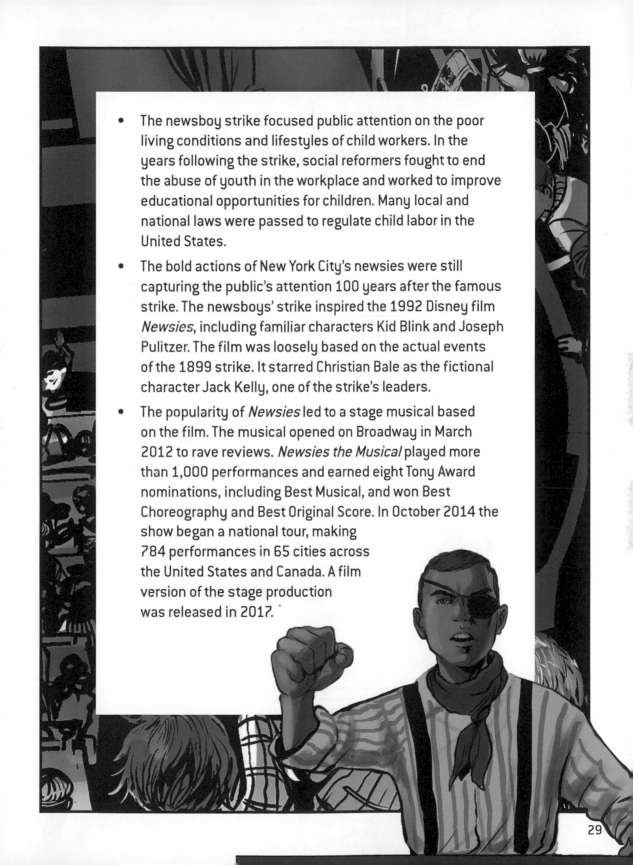

- The newsboy strike focused public attention on the poor living conditions and lifestyles of child workers. In the years following the strike, social reformers fought to end the abuse of youth in the workplace and worked to improve educational opportunities for children. Many local and national laws were passed to regulate child labor in the United States.

- The bold actions of New York City's newsies were still capturing the public's attention 100 years after the famous strike. The newsboys' strike inspired the 1992 Disney film *Newsies*, including familiar characters Kid Blink and Joseph Pulitzer. The film was loosely based on the actual events of the 1899 strike. It starred Christian Bale as the fictional character Jack Kelly, one of the strike's leaders.

- The popularity of *Newsies* led to a stage musical based on the film. The musical opened on Broadway in March 2012 to rave reviews. *Newsies the Musical* played more than 1,000 performances and earned eight Tony Award nominations, including Best Musical, and won Best Choreography and Best Original Score. In October 2014 the show began a national tour, making 784 performances in 65 cities across the United States and Canada. A film version of the stage production was released in 2017.

GLOSSARY

assemblyman (uh-SEM-blee-man)—a member of a legislative body in government

compromise (KAHM-pruh-myz)—a settlement in which each side gives up part of its demands and agrees to the final product

distribution (dis-tri-BYOO-shun)—having to do with giving things out

ethnicity (eth-NIH-sit-ee)—a group of people who share similar physical features, beliefs, and backgrounds

financial (fye-NAN-chul)—having to do with money

hawk (HAWK)—to sell something, especially by offering goods on the street or some other public place

immigrant (IM-uh-gruhnt)—someone who comes from one country to live permanently in another country

indispensable (in-dih-SPEN-suh-buhl)—absolutely necessary

journalism (JUR-nuhl-iz-uhm)—the work of gathering and reporting news for newspapers, magazines, and TV

orphan (OR-fuhn)—a child whose parents are not alive

publisher (PUHB-lish-er)—someone who makes and sells printed things such as newspapers or books

resolution (rez-uh-LOO-shuhn)—a firm decision to do something

scab (SKAB)—a person who refuses to strike or to join a labor union

soak (SOHK)—to beat severely

trolley (TRAH-lee)—an electric streetcar that runs on tracks and gets its power from an overhead wire

READ MORE

Long, Michael G. *Kids on the March: 15 Stories of Speaking Out, Protesting, and Fighting for Justice.* Chapel Hill, NC: Algonquin Young Readers, 2021.

Sohn, Emily. *National Woman's Party: Fight for Suffrage.* North Mankato, MN: Capstone Press, 2021.

Yomtov, Nel. *School Strike for Climate.* North Mankato, MN: Capstone Press, 2022.

INTERNET SITES

Blast from the Past: Newsboy Strike of 1899
nyhistory.org/blogs/blast-from-the-past-newsboy-strike-of-1899

History of the Newsboys or Newsies Strike of 1899 for Kids
bedtimehistorystories.com/newsboys-newsies-strike-of-1899-for-kids

July 20, 1899: Newsboys Strike
zinnedproject.org/news/tdih/newsboys-strike

ABOUT THE AUTHOR

photo by Nancy Golden

Nel Yomtov is an award-winning author of children's nonfiction books and graphic novels. He specializes in writing about history, current events, biography, architecture, and military history. He has written numerous graphic novels for Capstone, including the recent *School Strike for Climate*, *Journeying to New Worlds: A Max Axiom Super Scientist Adventure*, and *Cher Ami: Heroic Carrier Pigeon of World War I*. In 2020 he self-published *Baseball 100*, an illustrated book featuring the 100 greatest players in baseball history. Nel lives in the New York City area.

ABOUT THE ILLUSTRATOR

photo by Silvio dB

Silvio dB is a comic book artist from Brazil. He has illustrated numerous graphic novels for Capstone, including *Cleansing the World: Flood Myths Around the World*, *Vikings: Scandinavia's Ferocious Sea Raiders*, *Ninjas: Japan's Stealthy Secret Agents*, and *Nat Turner's Rebellion*.